Poems to the Homeless

Tina Whalen

Poems to the Homeless
Copyright © 2020 by Tina Whalen

All rights reserved. No part of this publication may
be reproduced, distributed, or transmitted in any
form or by any means, including photocopying,
recording, or other electronic or mechanical
methods, without the prior written permission of
the author, except in the case of brief quotations
embodied in critical reviews and certain other
non-commercial uses permitted by copyright law.

Tellwell Talent
www.tellwell.ca

ISBN
978-0-2288-4453-2 (Hardcover)
978-0-2288-4452-5 (Paperback)

Table of Contents

Introduction 1
Broken Systems 3
Threads 4
Canada 5
Christmas Day Shadow 6
The Days That Were 7
Inner Beauty 8
Even the Birds… 9
Shirley 10
Hostile Elements 11
Emergency 12
Night Watch 13
Meals 14
Cry Alone 15
Robert 16
Are You Happy? 17
Changes 18

Introduction

I wrote *Poems to the Homeless* in 1999, during the most vulnerable time in my life, a special time when I understood my own and other people's sufferings and vulnerabilities. It was a time when my heart empathized greatly with uninvited or inevitable loss and trauma. It was a time when I could reach out and heal others a little–as well as myself–with all the passion and feelings of injustice that welled up in me and for the victims of failed systems. I did not judge them.

Writing these poems helped me forget my own pain. I reached out physically, emotionally, and spiritually to the people mentioned in the poems. These people were real! I saw them on bitter winter nights as they slept on the streets of Toronto. I fed them with warm food and clothed them with blankets. I talked to each of them as a friend and touched them. I did not lose my way, but I could tell they had lost all their fighting power, hope, and well-being.

That could be me, I said in *Broken Systems* – one of the poems in this collection. It could be any of us. No one knows if one day, we might need the kindness of strangers.

Tina Whalen
1999

Broken Systems

No one can help.
How could that be?

The law says…
something about *free will*…
after seventy-two hours, release?'

Oh! Please! they say,
*they choose to live like that
on the street!*

No guarantee -
that could be me… or you

Six o'clock news

>   *bring your dogs in
>   it will be freezing tonight*

Threads

Threads
that bind us –
to each other

Aid that goes at every hour
aid to Colombia
aid to Kosovo
aid to Winnipeg
aid to Quebec
aides everywhere

To aid the world
since we have more

not on the list…

Canada's homeless.

How does the proverb go?
charity begins at home – you know?

Eh?

Canada

Inspires the world
the United Nations
a notion…

Canada is compassionate
Just
Fair
Generous
Responsible
Caring

Each and every Canadian
street person
could have told you.

Christmas Day Shadow

Snow falling gently
beautifully…

A cold, lonely creature
sneaker-clad
making imprints rather bold

A grocery cart
stubborn -
        not moving

Patiently pushing
one foot
        the other foot
on the bottom bar

Strain, progress
inch by inch

Come and eat
and warm yourself with us
NO ONE SAID.

The Days That Were

She was a lady
of high society
Rich, beautiful
Learned, famous
And now...*a tragedy.*

Traces burst from every pore
of the days that were...

Now - a schizophrenic
yet, eloquence still clings to her
intelligent eyes
refined taste
somewhat shattered still

Feels shame and sorrow
Yells with rage she can't control.

Inner Beauty

Matted hair
Like the hairball that
Cats swallow and bring up
Brown hands
From dirt
Broken, dirty fingernails
And no teeth for chewing
Not much to chew
Not much to look at when nature calls
And passersby
Look the other way

A penny for your thoughts…

Even the Birds...

She bought the birds a cookie
from Starbucks

This is for the birds
she said
and threw it on the ground

Her heart could still feel
Sympathy and Care
But...
NOT FOR PEOPLE!

Shirley

She's happy with the *feel*
of elegance
from Escada

With the *smell*
of coffee
from Starbucks

With the *sight*
of books
from Chapters

Part of her world now
Window shopping!
Riches gone - rags left

Hostile Elements

Rain is falling…
her blankets wet
at the tip
under the   overhang

It happened before -
Soaked
Drenched
Smelly
Uninhabitable

Nowhere to lie down
pace the ground

ONE A.M., TWO A.M., THREE A.M.
Where is ANYBODY!
Screams echo in –
        the empty street

Emergency

Stormy winter
snow piled   high
Street Help visits

Shelters nearby
army in sight
things are all right

Twenty minus - get inside
I don't want to
will die with pride

Manpower ready
shovel streets
around the homeless in big heaps

Here's a blanket
here's some coffee
here's a sandwich

Just sit tight!

Night Watch

I watch her from my window
every moment of the day
                      and night

Smoking cigarettes…alone
hungry, crazy, wild
circling, quiet, subdued
puzzling, strong, brave

HERO!

Unacclaimed   unsung
strained gaze

Up and down for
a voice
food, drink
shelter
a human touch

She waits…

Meals

Half-empty coffee cups
left on top of city bins
good to the last drop

Half-eaten hamburgers
taste good too

And some soft drinks
left behind

Pennies from change slots
and cigarette butts

TREASURES!

Cry Alone

Furiously - the storm
stole each piece
covers, papers
a paper sign

Begging for money
a shirt, then another shirt
a hat, a scarf
a sweater, a sock
EVERYTHING

A lonely voice screams
A furious body twists
That's all I have

STOP! STOP! STOP!

SILENCE

Robert

Like a child, he sat for months
under the Old Yorkville Cinema
and tried to sleep
a restless sleep

It was his home…

He was polite
humble, desperate
he had a puppet friend
that helped him beg

Drug traffickers
became his *friends*
kept him up at night
secretly using, abusing him

And - a policeman said
KILLED HIM

Are You Happy?

*If you're happy
and you know it
spare some change*
He repeats on and on
every day to everyone.

Smiles and songs
all day long
childlike talk
inner hope.

*If you're happy
and you know it
spare some change*

Or
smile back.

Changes

Dogs are fine
Humans should be too
Change the LAW
Change the HEART
Change the BRAIN
Change PHILOSOPHY
Change SELF
Change OFFICIALS

Take POWER
And make a BETTER WORLD…
NOW!

www.ingramcontent.com/pod-product-compliance
Lightning Source LLC
LaVergne TN
LVHW091935070526
838200LV00069B/1886